snapshot·picture·library

DIGGING MACHINES

snapshot•picture•library

DIGGING MACHINES

FOG CITY PRESS

Published by Fog City Press,
a division of Weldon Owen Inc.
415 Jackson Street
San Francisco, CA 94111 USA
www.weldonowen.com

WELDON OWEN INC.
Executive Chairman, Weldon Owen Group John Owen
President, CEO Terry Newell
Senior VP, International Sales Stuart Laurence
VP, Sales and New Business Development Amy Kaneko
VP, Publisher Roger Shaw
VP, Creative Director Gaye Allen
Executive Editor Elizabeth Dougherty
Assistant Editor Sarah Gurman
Designer William Mack
Production Director Chris Hemesath
Production Manager Michelle Duggan
Color Manager Teri Bell

A WELDON OWEN PRODUCTION
© 2008 Weldon Owen Inc.

Library of Congress Control Number: 2008935245

ISBN-13: 978-1-74089-855-3

10 9 8 7 6 5 4 3 2 1

Color separations by Sang Choy International, Singapore.
Printed by Tien Wah Press in Singapore.

Have you ever watched digging machines hard at work? Whether building houses or highways, we need diggers' powerful arms for many important jobs.

With tools like large buckets and jackhammers, diggers can tackle any scooping, hauling, or smashing project out there. Let's dig in and watch these mighty machines in action!

A front-end loader
scoops from the
front with its
large bucket.

These backhoes
have digging
buckets that
sweep down and
back toward
the cabin.

Mini diggers work on small jobs or in places where larger diggers can't fit.

Skid steer loaders are also good in small spaces because they can make tight turns.

This backhoe has a front bucket. It can scoop from the front and dig from the back at the same time!

The driver sits in the cabin and uses levers and buttons to move the digger.

Big wheels or tracks keep diggers from getting stuck in the mud.

When diggers
rotate and
swing their long
arm, they can
reach out in
any direction.

The bucket has "teeth" to bite into the ground and claw up the earth.

The teeth make
digging a huge
hole like this
an easy job!

Hydraulic cylinders move a digger's arm, which is called the boom.

Some machines have special arm attachments. The giant claw for grabbing is called a thumb.

Farmers use diggers every day out in the fields. It takes a lot of digging and hauling to keep a farm running!

Diggers are very
good at digging
deep trenches.

With the help of
diggers, crews
can lay pipelines
for water or oil.

Diggers do
the heavy
lifting and
smashing on
road projects.

Diggers can also clear and flatten land, just like a bulldozer.

A digger's huge bucket can level ground and dig out basements for new houses.

Sometimes
diggers
tear down
something
old before
they build
something new.

Diggers often work in teams. One machine can't do the job alone!

These diggers
are making
room for the
foundations of
tall buildings.

Diggers are on call around the clock. The crew needs to finish the building on time!

Sometimes
diggers get
wet scooping
mud or sand
at a shoreline.

These giant
diggers work in
the coal mines.
It takes big
machines to get
this job done.

These machines
are drilling holes
in a gold mine.

Wherever they are, diggers work hard. It's nice when there are trucks to help carry the load, too!

And when one job is done, a digger is off again, riding on a trailer to its next adventure.

Front-end loader

Front-end loaders are good for moving large amounts of material from one place to another. The bucket is connected to the digger by two powerful arms.

Skid loader

The arms of a skid loader hinge on either side of the cabin. These diggers can turn in small circles, and they can even get into a hole and dig from inside!

Backhoe

Backhoes are the best machines for digging holes. The cabin and boom can rotate and reach in all directions. Most backhoes weigh between five and ten tons.

Backhoe loader

Backhoe loaders are a bit like tractors, but they have a shovel at the front and a boom and bucket at the back! They are good for fixing roads and building houses.

Mini digger

These are a smaller version of the backhoe. Mini diggers can weigh as little as one or two tons. They can even drive through a door and go inside a house!

Coal mine excavator

These large-scale diggers are used for coal mining. Huge wheels scrape into the earth, and then conveyor belts carry the loose material away for processing.

Cabin

This is where the driver sits and controls the digger. From up high in the cabin, the driver can see all around. There are also some remote-controlled diggers.

Chassis

The cabin of a backhoe or mini digger is mounted on a rotating chassis. This means it can swivel the cabin and boom around while the wheels stay in the same place.

Track

Tracked wheels evenly distribute the weight of diggers, which helps them move over rough and rocky ground, and keeps them from getting stuck in the mud.

Bucket

The bucket and teeth of a digger are extra strong so that it can rip up concrete and load rubble. Some buckets have extra cutters on the sides.

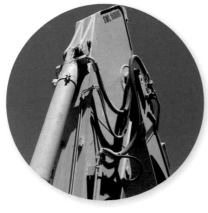

Boom

This is the "arm" of the digger. The boom is powered by hydraulics. This means that the pressure from water pushing through the pistons makes the boom move.

Attachments

If a bucket is not right for the job, diggers can use special attachments to help scoop out trenches, rip up concrete, and crush and flatten earth.

Acknowledgments

Weldon Owen would like to thank the staff at Toucan Books Ltd, London, for their assistance in the production of this book: Ellen Dupont, managing director; Hannah Bowen, author, project manager, and researcher; and Leah Germann, designer.